GREAT DUN

d. blue

Living in the 1950s

Rosemary Rees & Judith Maguire

Heinemann Library,
an imprint of Heinemann Publishers (Oxford) Ltd,
Halley Court, Jordan Hill, Oxford, OX2 8EJ

OXFORD LONDON EDINBURGH
MADRID PARIS ATHENS BOLOGNA
MELBOURNE SYDNEY AUCKLAND
SINGAPORE TOKYO IBADAN
NAIROBI GABORONE HARARE
PORTSMOUTH NH (USA)

© Heinemann Library 1993

First published 1993
93 94 95 96   10 9 8 7 6 5 4 3 2 1

British Library Cataloguing in Publication Data
is available on request from the British Library.

ISBN 0 431 07215 9

Designed by Philip Parkhouse
Printed and bound in China

Acknowledgements
The authors and publisher would like to thank the following
for permission to reproduce photographs:
Advertising Archive: p. 21
Hulton Picture Company: pp. 7, 8, 12, 13, 15, 16, 17, 23, 26, 28, 29
Robert Opie Collection: p. 18
Popperfoto: pp. 6, 19, 20, 25, 27
Con Dawson: pp. 22, 24, 30
Topham: pp. 4, 5, 9, 10, 11, 14

Cover photograph: Hulton Picture Company

Contents

Home 1 — 4
Home 2 — 6
Home 3 — 8
School 1 — 10
School 2 — 12
Work 1 — 14
Work 2 — 16
Spare Time 1 — 18
Spare Time 2 — 20
Holidays 1 — 22
Holidays 2 — 24
Holidays 3 — 26
Special Days 1 — 28
Special Days 2 — 30

Time Line — 31
Index — 32

Home 1

These houses were built in the 1950s.
New houses had to be built after the war, as lots of houses had been bombed.
As many new houses were built, new towns and cities were made.
All the new houses had inside toilets.
Many of the old houses had their toilets in the back yard.

Most houses did not have fridges.
You kept your food cool in the larder.
Some houses had radios, but only a few had televisions.
Most of the furniture in a house was made of wood.
It had to be polished to keep it clean.

Home 2

When the war was over, there were many more sweets in the shops.
Some children spent all their money on sweets and ice creams.
Many sweets were kept in big jars.
The shopkeeper weighed them for you, and put them in a paper bag.

There was more food to buy after the war.
People could buy more sugar, so they made more cakes and biscuits.
People liked having afternoon tea.
Shops got bigger because there was more food to buy.
Many shops sold lots of different things.

Home 3

Most women did all their washing by hand.
Washing machines were still very new.
They were very big and very noisy.
People hung their washing in the street to dry.
Washing for a family took a long time.
It could take a whole day.

This was a new launderette.
You could wash and dry your clothes here.
It was faster than doing it by hand.
Now washing did not take all day.
Women did their washing with their friends.
They carried the washing home on the pram.

School 1

This school was new in 1954.
It was built for young children.
All young children had school milk every day.
If you were good, you were milk monitor.
Milk monitors looked after the milk bottles and the straws.

These boys and girls had to wash their hands after playtime.
At playtime the girls played skipping.
They also played 'Farmer's in his den', and 'Oranges and Lemons'.
Both the boys and the girls played marbles.
Boys played football on the playground.

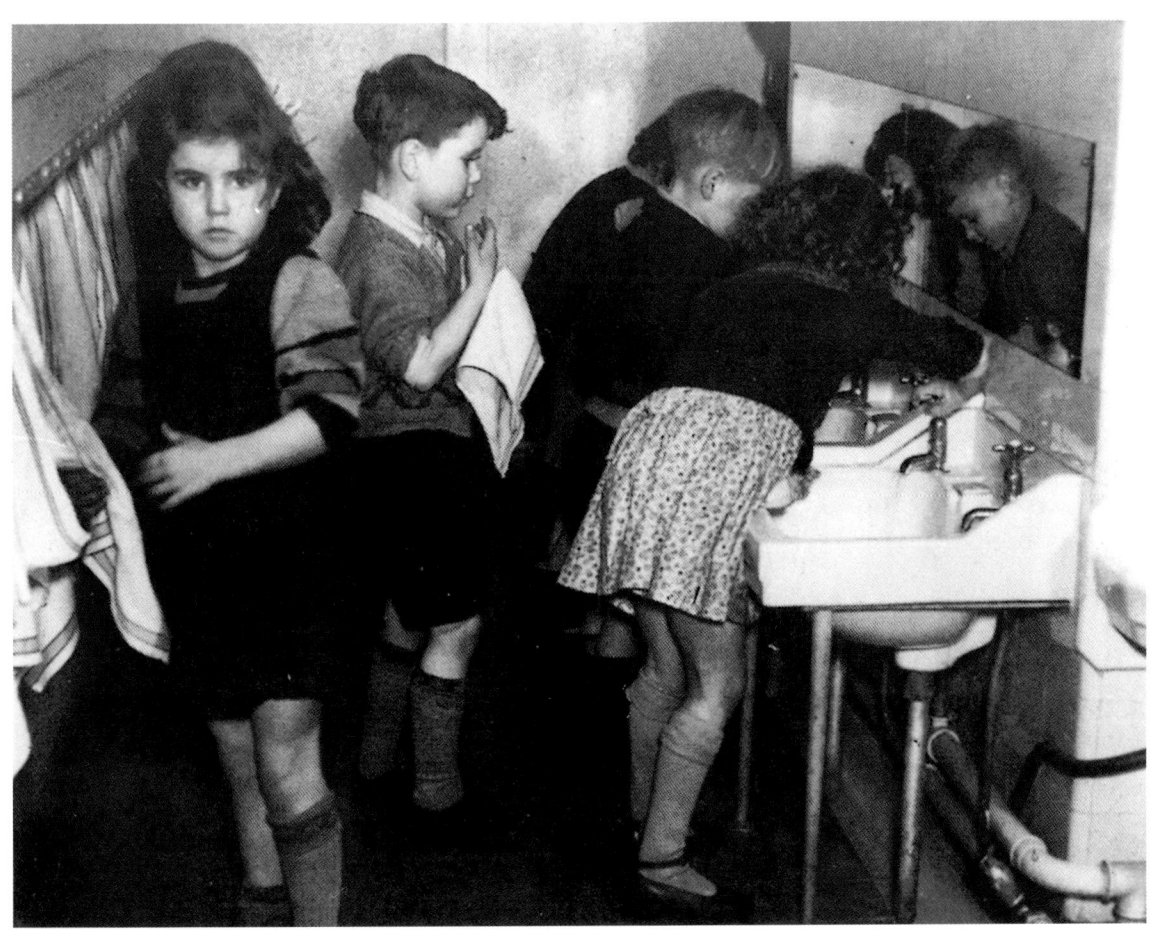

School 2

When children were 11, they did a big test in school.
In school you had to work very hard to learn lots of things for the test.
After children did the test, they were told which new school they would go to.
Children did not always go to the same school as their friends.

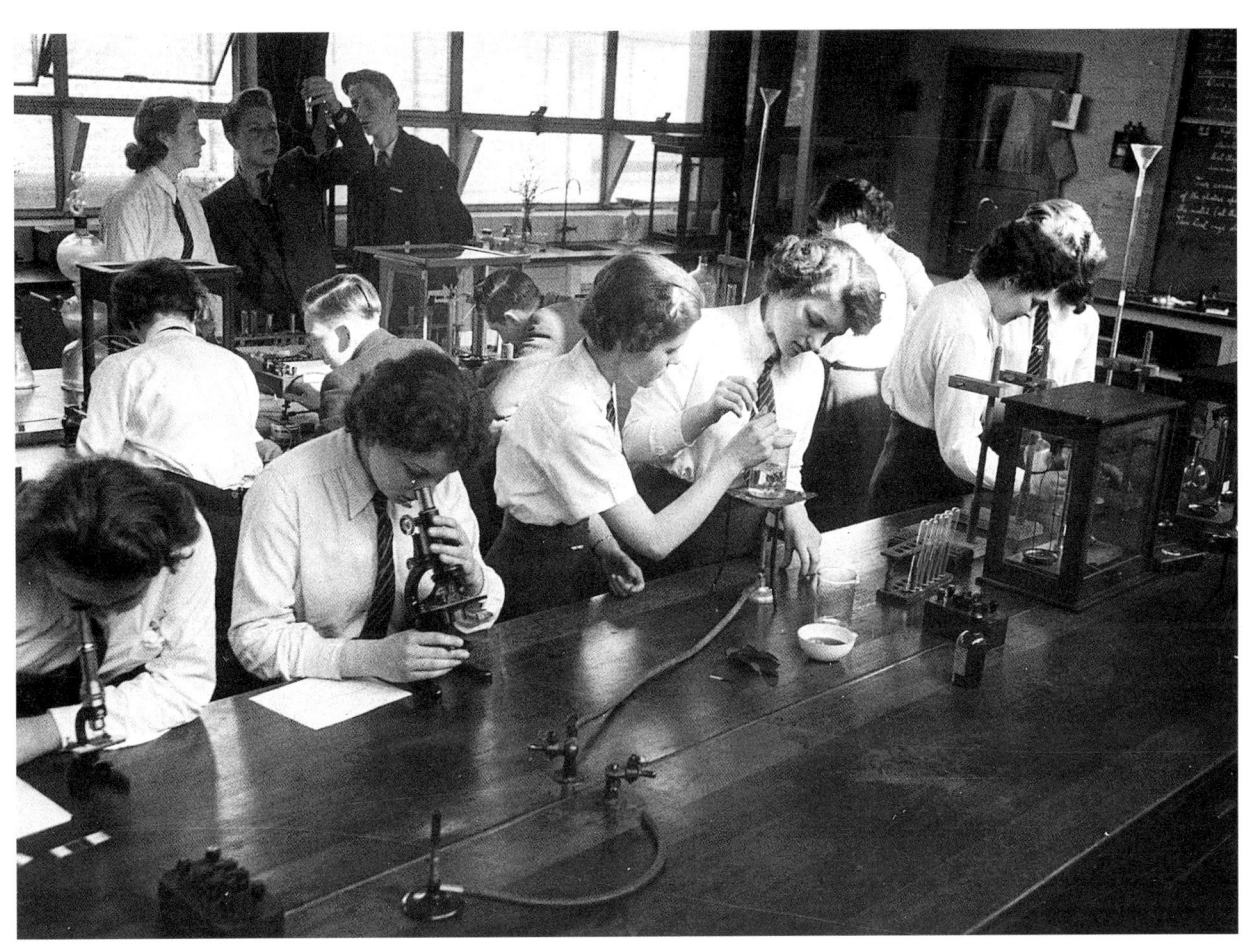

These older children all wore the same
sort of clothes to school.
It is called a uniform.
They all wore shirts and ties.
The girls wore grey skirts.
The boys had to wear short trousers until
they were 14. Then they could wear
long trousers.

Work 1

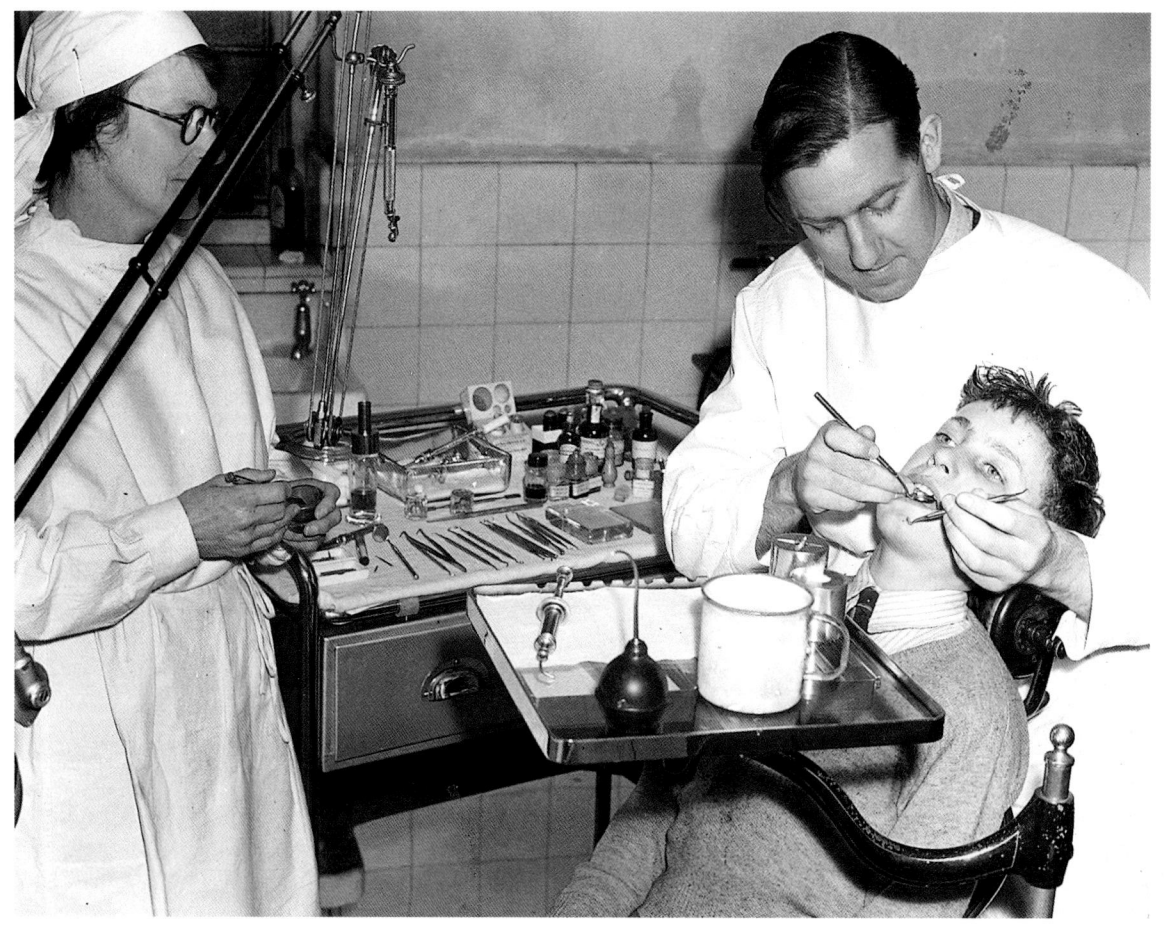

This boy had to go to the dentist.
Going to the dentist could hurt a lot.
The dentist did not give you anything to stop it hurting.
Lots of children ate too many sweets. This made their teeth bad.
Children did not like going to the dentist.

These men worked on the fishing boats.
They spent nearly three weeks out at sea.
If they caught lots of fish, they got paid well.
If they did not catch any fish, they did not get paid.
It was their job to clean and sort the fish when they got back to shore.

Work 2

These men were miners.
They had to dig coal from underground.
They used pit ponies to pull the coal out in little trucks.
The ponies stayed underground nearly all year.
In the summer, the ponies had a holiday in the sunshine.

Many girls left school at 15 or 16 to get a job.
This woman got a job in an office.
She went to college to learn to type and take notes.
She could type 100 words in one minute.
She stopped working when she got married.

Spare Time 1

Lots of children read comics.
Some of the comics were for boys,
like 'The Eagle'.
Some of the comics were for girls, like
'School Friend'.
Some comics were for boys and girls,
like 'Swift'.

'Muffin the Mule' was a children's television programme.
Not many families had a television.
If you did not have a television, you may have watched it at a friend's house.
People liked watching television.
Soon lots of people started to buy them.

Spare time 2

This man and woman are dancing.
Lots of people had lessons to learn how to dance.
They would listen to records.
The dances they learnt were called the tango, the foxtrot and the jive.
At night, many people would go to dance halls to dance with their friends.

In the 1950s there were fewer cars on the roads than there are today.
People cycled to work and cycled for fun.
Lots of people enjoyed cycling.

Holidays 1

These children went on holiday to the seaside.
More people started to take holidays every year.
These children had spades to dig with.
The spades were made of metal and wood.
Their mums and dads sat on wooden deckchairs on the beach.

Many people went on holiday by train.
It could take a long time to get there.
Trains were slower than they are today.
This little girl is coming back from holiday.
Sometimes, it was better to travel at night.
It cost less, and the trains were not so busy.

Holidays 2

These children went on holiday to a farm.
They had fun on the farm, looking after the animals and playing with them.
They could not play on the big machines, but they saw how they worked.
They had fresh eggs and milk every day.

Some families went to holiday camps.
Holiday camps were a new idea.
There were things for mums, dads and children to do.
The children liked them because they could have fun without mum and dad.
Mums and dads liked them because the children were happy.

Holidays 3

This was Blackpool in the 1950s.
Lots of people went to Blackpool on holiday. It had a good beach and lots of things to do.
These women are eating candyfloss.
There were lots of shops and places to eat.
There was a fun fair and lots of places to play.

Some people spent their holiday in a caravan.
Friends would go together.
There were not many caravan sites to visit.
Lots of people stayed on farms.
If you stayed at a farm, you had to use the bathroom in the farmhouse.

Special Days 1

This family went to a big festival in London.

Lots of new buildings were built for the festival.

The buildings were painted in bright colours.

They were not just made of bricks and stone. Some were made of metal.

The Queen was crowned in 1953.
She went from the palace in a big gold coach.
Lots of people went to watch.
It was a very happy day.
Some people had parties at home or in the streets.

Special Days 2

These girls were at a birthday party.
It was warm, so they played outside.
They played 'Oranges and Lemons'.
They had lots of fun.
All the girls wore new party
dresses and ribbons in their hair.

Time Line

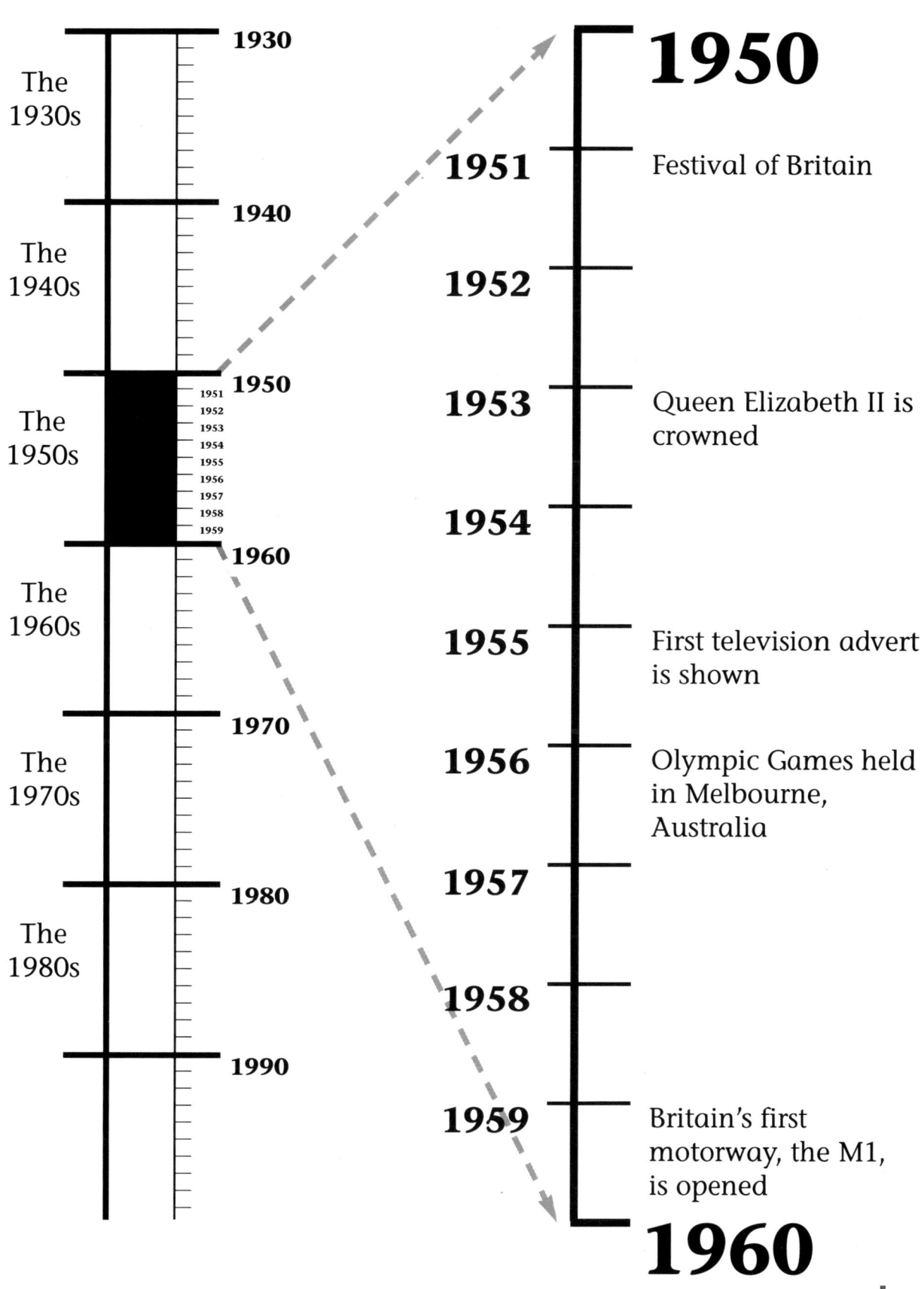

31

Index

	page
birthdays	30
cars	21
comics	18
dentist	4
football	11
holidays	22, 23, 24, 25, 26, 27
houses	4 – 5
playtime	11
school	10, 11 – 13
sweets	16, 14
television	5, 19
washing	8, 9